The Rape of the Lock

ALEXANDER POPE

Catherine

A classy

chick.

love –

Dave

A Phoenix Paperback

This abridged edition published in 1996 by Phoenix
a division of Orion Books Ltd
Orion House, 5 Upper St Martin's Lane, London WC2H 9EA

Cover illustration: Detail from *The Reconcilliation of Oberon and Titania*,
by Joseph Noel Paton (Bridgeman Art Library, London)

ISBN 1 85799 672 0

Typeset by Deltatype Ltd, Ellesmere Port, Cheshire
Printed and bound in Great Britain by
Clays Ltd, St Ives plc

Contents

from An Essay on Criticism

A little Learning is a dang'rous Thing;
Drink deep, or taste not the Pierian Spring:
There shallow Draughts intoxicate the Brain,
And drinking largely sobers us again.
Fir'd at first Sight with what the Muse imparts,
In fearless Youth we tempt the Heights of Arts,
While from the bounded Level of our Mind,
Short Views we take, nor see the Lengths behind,
But more advanc'd, behold with strange Surprize
New, distant Scenes of endless Science rise!
So pleas'd at first, the towring Alps we try,
Mount o'er the Vales, and seem to tread the Sky,
Th' Eternal Snows appear already past,
And the first Clouds and Mountains seem the last:
But those attain'd, we tremble to survey
The growing Labours of the lengthen'd Way,
Th' increasing Prospect tires our wandring Eyes,
Hills peep o'er Hills, and Alps on Alps arise!
A perfect Judge will read each Work of Wit
With the same Spirit that its Autor writ,
Survey the Whole, nor seek slight Faults to find,
Where Nature moves, and Rapture warms the M'
Nor lose, for that malignant dull Delight,

The gen'rous Pleasure to be charm'd with Wit.
But in such Lays as neither ebb, nor flow,
Correctly cold, and regularly low,
That shunning Faults, one quiet Tenour keep;
We cannot blame indeed – but we may sleep.
In Wit, as Nature, what affects our Hearts
Is not th' Exactness of peculiar Parts;
'Tis not a Lip , or Eye we Beauty call,
But the joint Force and full Result of all.
Thus when we view some well-proportion'd Dome,
(The World's just Wonder, and ev'n thine O Rome!)
No single Parts unequally surprize;
All comes united to th' admiring Eyes;
No monstrous Height, or Breadth, or Length appear;
The Whole at once is Bold, and Regular.

  Whoever thinks a faultless Piece to see,
Thinks what ne'er was, nor is, nor e'er shall be.
In ev'ry Work regard the Writer's End,
Since none can compass more than they Intend;
And if the Means be just, the Conduct true,
Applause, in spite of trivial Faults, is due.
As Men of Breeding, sometimes Men of Wit,
T' avoid great Errors, must the less commit,
Neglect the Rules each Verbal Critick lays,
For not to know some Trifles, is a Praise.
Most Criticks, fond of some subservient Art,
Still make the Whole depend upon a Part,
They talk of Principles, but Notions prize,

And All to one lov'd Folly Sacrifice.

Once on a time, La Mancha's Knight, they say,
A certain Bard encountring on the Way,
Discours'd in Terms as just, with Looks as Sage,
As e'er cou'd Dennis, of the Grecian Stage;
Concluding all were desp'rate Sots and Fools,
Who durst depart from Aristotle's Rules.
Our Author, happy in a Judge so nice,
Produc'd his Play, and beg'd the Knight's Advice,
Made him observe the Subject and the Plot,
The Manners, Passions, Unities, what not?
All which, exact to Rule were brought about,
Were but a Combate in the Lists left out.
What! Leave the Combate out? Exclaims the Knight;
Yes, or we must renounce the Stagyrite.
Not so by Heav'n (he answers in a Rage)
Knights, Squires, and Steeds, must enter on the Stage,
So vast a Throng the Stage can ne'er contain.
Then build a New, or act it in a Plain.

Thus Criticks, of less Judgment than Caprice,
Curious, not Knowing, not exact, but nice,
From short Ideas; and offend in Arts
(As most in Manners) by a Love to Parts.

Some to Conceit alone their Taste confine,
And glitt'ring Thoughts struck out at ev'ry Line;
Pleas'd with a Work where nothing's just or fit;
One glaring Chaos and wild Heap of Wit:
Poets like Painters, thus, unskill'd to trace

3

The naked Nature and the living Grace,
With Gold and Jewels cover ev'ry Part,
And hide with Ornaments their Want of Art.
True Wit is Nature to Advantage drest,
What oft was Thought, but ne'er so well Exprest,
Something, whose Truth convinc'd at Sight we find,
That gives us back the Image of our Mind:
As Shades more sweetly recommend the Light,
So modest Plainness sets off sprightly Wit:
For Works may have more Wit than does 'em good,
As Bodies perish through Excess of Blood.

Others for Language all their Care express,
And value Books, as Women Men, for Dress:
Their Praise is still – The Stile is excellent:
The Sense, they humbly take upon Content.
Words are like Leaves; and where they most abound,
Much Fruit of Sense beneath is rarely found.
False Eloquence, like the Prismatic Glass,
Its gawdy Colours spread on ev'ry place;
The Face of Nature we no more Survey,
All glares alike, without Distinction gay:
But true Expression, like th' unchanging Sun,
Clears, and improves whate'er it shines upon,
It gilds all Objects, but it alters none.
Expression is the Dress of Thought, and still
Appears more decent as more suitable;
A vile Conceit in pompous Words exprest,
Is like a Clown in regal Purple drest;

For diff'rent Styles with diff'rent Subjects sort,
As several Garbs with Country, Town, and Court,
Some by Old Words to Fame have made Pretence;
With sharpen'd sight pale Antiquaries pore,
Th' inscription value, but the rust adore;
This the blue varnish, that the green endears,
The sacred rust of twice ten hundred years!
To gain Pescennius one employs his schemes,
One grasps a Cecrops in ecstatic dreams;
Poor Vadius, long with learned spleen devour'd,
Can taste no pleasure since his Shield was scour'd;
And Curio, restless by the Fair-one's side,
Sighs for an Otho, and neglects his bride.

Theirs is the Vanity, the Learning thine:
Touch'd by thy land, again Rome's glories shine,
Her Gods, and god-like Heroes rise to view,
And all her faded garlands bloom a-new.
Nor blush, these studies thy regard engage;
These pleas'd the Fathers of poetic rage;
The verse and sculpture bore an equal part,
And Art reflected images to Art.

Oh when shall Britain, conscious of her claim,
Stand emulous of Greek and Roman fame?
In living medals see her wars enroll'd,
And vanquish'd realms supply recording gold?
Here, rising bold, the Patriot's honest face;
There Warriors frowning in historic brass:
Then future ages with delight shall see

How Plato's, Bacon's, Newton's looks agree;
Or in fair series laurell'd Bards be shown,
A Virgil there, and here an Addison.
Then shall thy CRAGS (and let me call him mine)
On the cast ore, another Pollio, shine;
With aspect open, shall erect his head,
And round the orb in lasting notes be read,
'Statesman, yet friend to Truth! of soul sincere,
In action faithful, and in honour clear;
Who broke no promise, serv'd no private end,
Who gain'd no title, and who lost no friend,
Ennobled by himself, by all approv'd,
And prais'd, unenvy'd, by the Muse he lov'd.'

The Rape of the Lock

CANTO I

What dire Offence from am'rous Causes springs,
What mighty Contents rise from trivial Things,
I sing – This Verse to Caryll, Muse! is due;
This, ev'n Belinda may vouchsafe to view:
Slight is the Subject, but not so the Praise,
If She inspire, and he approve my Lays,
　　Say what strange Motive, Goddess! cou'd compel
A well-bred Lord t'assault a gentle Belle?
Oh say what stranger Cause, yet unexplor'd,

Cou'd make a gentle Belle reject a Lord?
In Tasks so bold, can Little Men engage,
And in soft Bosoms dwells such mighty Rage?

  Sol thro' white Curtains shot a tim'rous Ray,
And op'd those Eyes that must eclipse the Day;
Now Lapdogs give themselves the rowzing Shake,
And sleepless Lovers, just at Twelve, awake:
Thrice rung the Bell, the Slipper knock'd the Ground,
And the press'd Watch return'd a silver Sound.
Belinda still her downy Pillow prest,
Her Guardian Sylph prolong'd the balmy Rest.
'Twas he had summon'd to her silent Bed
The Morning-Dream that hover'd o'er her Head.
A Youth more glitt'ring than a Birth-night Beau,
(That ev'n in Slumber caus'd her Cheek to glow)
Seem'd to her Ear has winning Lips to lay,
And thus in Whispers said, or seem'd to say.

  Fairest of Mortals, thou distinguish'd Care
Of thousand bright Inhabitants of Air!
If e'er one Vision touch'd thy infant Thought,
Of all the Nurse and all the Priest have taught,
Of airy Elves by Moonlight Shadows seen,
The silver Token, and the circled Green,
Or Virgins visited by Angel-Pow'rs,
With Golden Crowns and Wreaths of heavn'ly Flow'rs,
Hear and believe! thy own Importance know,
Nor bound thy narrow Views to Things below.
Some secret Truths from Learned Pride conceal'd,

To Maids alone and Children are reveal'd:
What tho' no Credit doubting Wits may give?
The Fair and Innocent shall still believe.
Know then, unnumber'd Spirits round thee fly,
The light Militia of the lower Sky;
These, tho' unseen, are ever on the Wing,
Hang o'er the Box, and hover round the Ring.
Think what an Equipage thou hast in Air,
And view with scorn Two Pages and a Chair.
As now your own, our Beings were of old,
And once inclos'd in Woman's beauteous Mold;
Thence, by a soft Transition, we repair
From earthly Vehicles to these of Air.
Think not, when Woman's transient Breath is fled,
That all her Vanities at once are dead:
Succeeding Vanities she still regards,
And tho' she play no more, o'erlooks the Cards.
Her Joy in gilded Chariots, when alive,
And Love of Ombre, after Death survive.
For when the Fair in all their Pride expire,
To their first Elements their Souls retire:
The Sprights of fiery Termagants in Flame
Mount up, and take a Salamander's Name.
Soft yielding Minds to Water glide away,
And sip with Nymphs, their Elemental Tea.
The graver Prude sinks downward to a Gnome,
In search of Mischief still on Earth to roam.
The light Coquettes in Sylphs aloft repair,

And sport and flutter in the Fields of Air.

    Know farther yet; Whoever fair and chaste
Rejects Mankind, is by some Sylph embrac'd:
For Spirits, freed from mortal Laws, with ease
Assume what Sexes and what Shapes they please.
What guards the Purity of melting Maids,
In Courtly Balls, and Midnight Masquerades,
Safe from the treach'rous Friend, the daring Spark,
The Glance by Day, the Whisper in the Dark;
When kind Occasion prompts their warm Desires.
When Musick softens, and when Dancing fires?
'Tis but their Sylph, he wise Celestials know,
Tho' Honour is the Word with Men below.

    Some Nymphs there are, too conscious of their Face,
For Life predestin'd to the Gnomes' Embrace,
These swell their Prospects and exalt their Pride,
When Offers are disdain'd, and Love deny'd.
They gay Ideas crowd the vacant Brain;
While Peers and Dukes, and all their sweeping Train,
And Garters, Stars and Coronets appear,
And in soft Sounds, Your Grace salutes their Ear.
'Tis these that early taint the Female Soul,
Instruct the Eyes of young Coquettes to roll,
Teach Infant-Cheeks a bidden Blush to know,
And little Hearts to flutter at a Beau.

    Oft when the World imagine Women stray,
The Sylphs thro' mystick Mazes guide their Way,
Thro' all the giddy Circle they pursue,

And old Impertinence expel by new.
What tender Maid but must a Victim fall
To one Man's Treat, but for another's Ball?
When Florio speaks, what Virgin could withstand,
If gentle Damon did not squeeze her Hand?
With varying Vanities, from ev'ry Part,
They shift the moving Toyshop of their Heart;
Where Wigs with Wigs, with Sword-knots Sword-knots
    strive,
Beaus banish Beaus, and Coaches Coaches drive.
This erring Mortals Levity may call,
Oh blind to Truth! the Sylphs contrive it all.

    Of these am I, who thy Protection claim,
A watchful Sprite, and Ariel is my Name.
Late, as I rang'd the Crystal Wilds of Air,
In the clear Mirror of thy ruling Star
I saw, alas! some dread Event impend,
Ere to the Main this Morning Sun descend.
But Heav'n reveals not what, or how, or where:
Warn'd by thy Sylph, oh Pious Maid beware!
This to disclose is all thy Guardian can.
Beware of all, but most beware of Man!

    He said; when Shock, who thought she slept too long,
Leapt up, and wak'd his Mistress with his Tongue.
'Twas then Belinda! if Report say true,
Thy Eyes first open'd on a Billet-doux;
Wounds, Charms, and Ardors, were no sooner read,
But all the Vision vanish'd from thy Head.

And now, unveil'd, the Toilet stands display'd,
Each Silver Vase in mystic Order laid.
First, rob'd in White, the Nymph intent adores
With Head uncover'd, the Cosmetic Pow'rs.
A heav'nly Image in the Glass appears,
To that she bends, to that her Eyes she rears;
Th'inferior Priestess, at her Altar's side,
Trembling, begins the sacred Rites of Pride.
Unnumber'd Treasures ope at once, and here
The various Off'rings of the World appear;
From each she nicely culls with curious Toil,
And decks the Goddess with the glitt'ring Spoil.
This Casket India's glowing Gems unlocks,
And all Arabia breathes from yonder Box.
The Tortoise here and Elephant unite,
Transform'd to Combs, the speckled and the white.
Here Files of Pins extend their shining Rows,
Puffs, Powders, Patches, Bibles, Billet-doux.
Now awful Beauty put on all its Arms;
The Fair each moment rises in her Charms,
Repairs her Smiles, awakens ev'ry Grace,
And calls forth all the Wonders of her Face;
Sees by Degrees a purer Blush arise,
And keener Lightnings quicken in her Eyes.
The busy Sylphs surround their darling Care;
These set the Head, and those divide the Hair,
Some fold the Sleeve, whilst others plait the Gown;
And Betty's prais'd for Labours not her own.

Not with more Glories, in th' Etherial Plain,
The Sun first rises o'er the purpled Main,
Than issuing forth, the Rival of his Beams
Lanch'd on the Bosom of the Silver Thames.
Fair Nymphs, and well-drest Youths around her shone,
But ev'ry Eye was fix'd on her alone.
On her white Breast a sparkling Cross she wore,
Which Jews might kiss, and Infidels adore.
Her lively Looks a sprightly Mind disclose,
Quick as her Eyes, and as unfix'd as those:
Favours to none, to all the Smiles extends,
Oft she rejects, but never once offends,
Bright as the Sun, her eyes the Gazers strike,
And, like the Sun, they shine on all alike.
Yet graceful Ease, and Sweetness void of Pride,
Might hide her Faults, if Belles had Faults to hide:
If to her share some Female Errors fall,
Look on her Face, and you'll forget 'em all.

This Nymph, to the Destruction of Mankind,
Nourish'd two Locks, which graceful hung behind
In equal Curls, and well conspir'd to deck
With shining Ringlets the smooth Iv'ry Neck.
Love in these Labyrinths his Slaves detains,
And mighty Hearts are held in slender Chains.
With hairy Sprindges we the Birds betray,
Slight Lines of Hair surprize the Finny Prey,
Fair Tresses Man's Imperial Race insnare,

And Beauty draws us with a single Hair.

Th' Adventrous Baron the bright Locks admir'd,
He saw, he wish'd, and to the Prize aspir'd:
Resolv'd to win, he meditates the way,
By Force to ravish, or by Fraud betray;
For when Success a Lover's Toil attends,
Few ask, if Fraud or Force attain'd his Ends.

For this, ere Phœbus rose, he had implor'd
Propitious Heav'n, and ev'ry Pow'r ador'd,
But chiefly Love – to Love an Altar built,
Of twelve vast French Romances, neatly gilt.
There lay three Garters, half a Pair of Gloves;
And all the Trophies of his former Loves.
With tender Billet-doux he light the Pyre,
And breathes three am'rous Sighs to raise the Fire.
Then prostrate falls, and begs with ardent Eyes
Soon to obtain, and long possess the Prize:
The Pow'rs gave Ear, and granted half his Pray'r,
The rest, the Winds dispers'd in empty Air.

But now secure the painted Vessel glides,
The Sun-beams trembling on the floating Tydes,
While melting Musick steals upon the Sky,
And soften'd Sounds along the Waters die.
Smooth flow the Waves, the Zephyrs gently play,
Belinda smil'd, and all the World was gay.
All but the Sylph – With careful Thoughts opprest,
The'impending Woe sate heavy on his Breast.
He summons strait his Denizens of Air;

13

The lucid Squadrons round the Sails repair:
Soft o'er the Shrouds Aerial Whispers breathe,
That seem'd but Zephyrs to the Train beneath.
Some to the Sun their Insect-Wings unfold,
Waft on the Breeze, or sink in Clouds of Gold.
Transparent Forms, too fine for mortal Sight,
Their fluid Bodies half dissolv'd in Light.
Loose to the Wind their airy Garments flew,
Thin glitt'ring Textures of the filmy Dew;
Dipt in the richest Tincture of the Skies,
Where Light disports in ever-mingling Dies,
While ev'ry Beam new transient Colours flings,
Colours that change whene'er they wave their Wings.
Amid the Circle, on the gilded Mast,
Superior by the Head, was Ariel plac'd;
His Purple Pinions opening to the Sun,
He rais'd his Azure Wand, and thus begun.

Ye Sylphs and Sylphids, to your Chief give Ear,
Fays, Fairies, Genii, Elves, and Dæmons hear!
Ye know the Spheres and various Tasks assign'd,
By Laws Eternal, to th' Aerial Kind.
Some in the Fields of purest Æther play,
And bask and whiten in the Blaze of day.
Some guide the Course of wandring Orbs on high,
Or roll the Planets thro' the boundless Sky.
Some less refin'd, beneath the Moon's pale Light
Pursue the Stars that shoot athwart the Night,
Or suck the Mists in grosser Air below,

Or dip their Pinions in the painted Bow,
Or brew fierce Tempests on the wintry Main,
Or o'er the Glebe distill the kindly Rain.
Others on Earth o'er human Race preside,
Watch all their Ways, and all their Actions guide:
Of these the Chief the Care of Nations own,
And guard with Arms Divine the British Throne.

Our humbler Province is to tend the Fair,
Not a less pleasing, tho' less glorious Care.
To save the Powder from too rude a Gale,
Nor let th' imprison'd Essences exhale,
To draw fresh Colours from the vernal Flow'rs,
To steal from Rainbows ere they drop in Show'rs
A brighter Wash; to curl their waving Hairs,
Assist their Blushes, and inspire their Airs;
Nay oft, in Dreams, Invention we bestow,
To change a Flounce, or add a Furbelo.

This Day, black Omens threat the brightest Fair
That e'er deserv'd a watchful Spirit's Care;
Some dire Disaster, or by Force, or Slight,
But what, or where, the Fates have wrapt in Night.
Whether the Nymph shall break Diana's Law,
Or some frail China Jar receive a Flaw,
Or stain her Honour, or her new Brocade,
Forget her Pray'rs, or miss a Masquerade,
Or lose her Heart, or Necklace, at a Ball;
Or whether Heav'n has doom'd and that Shock must fall.
Haste then ye Spirits! to your Charge repair;

The flutt'ring Fan be Zephyretta's Care;
The Drops to thee, Brillante, we consign;
And, Momentilla, let the Watch be thine;
Do thou, Crispissa, tend her fav'rite Lock;
Ariel himself shall be the Guard of Shock.

To Fifty chosen Sylphs, of special Note,
We trust th' important Charge, the Petticoat:
Oft have we known that sev'nfold Fence to fail,
Tho' stiff with Hoops, and arm'd with Ribs of Whale.
Form a strong Line about the Silver Bound,
And guard the wide Circumference around.

Whatever Spirit, careless of his Charge,
His Post neglects, or leaves the Fair at large,
Shall feel sharp Vengeance soon o'ertake his Sins,
Be stopt in Vials, or transfixt with Pins;
Or plung'd in Lakes of bitter Washes lie,
Or wedg'd whole Ages in a Bodkin's Eye:
Gums and Pomatums shall his Flight restrain,
While clog'd he beats his silken Wings in vain;
Or Alom-Stypticks with contracting Power
Shrink his thin Essence like a rivell'd Flower.
Or as Ixion fix'd, the Wretch shall feel
The giddy Motion of the whirling Mill,
In Fumes of burning Chocolate shall glow,
And tremble at the Sea that froaths below!

He spoke; the Spirits from the Sails descend;
Some, Orb in Orb, around the Nymph extend,
Some thrid the mazy Ringlets of her Hair,

Some hang upon the Pendants of her Ear;
With beating Hearts the dire Event they wait,
Anxious, and trembling for the Birth of Fate.

CANTO III

Close by those Meads for ever crown'd with Flow'rs,
Where Thames with Pride surveys his rising Tow'rs,
There stands a Structure of Majestick Frame,
Which from the neighb'ring Hampton takes its Name.
Here Britain's Statesmen oft the Fall foredoom
Of Foreign Tyrants, and of Nymphs at home;
Here Thou, Great Anna! whom three Realms obey,
Dost sometimes Counsel take – and sometimes Tea.

Hither the Heroes and the Nymphs resort,
To taste awhile the Pleasures of a Court;
In various Talk th' instructive hours they past,
Who gave the Ball, or paid the Visit last:
One speaks the Glory of the British Queen,
And one describes a charming Indian Screen;
And third interprets Motions, Looks, and Eyes;
At ev'ry Word a Reputation dies.
Snuff, or the Fan, supply each Pause of Chat,
With singing, laughing, ogling, and all that.

Mean while declining from the Noon of Day,
The Sun obliquely shoots his burning Ray;
The hungry Judges soon the Sentence sign,
And Wretches hang that Jury-men may Dine;
The Merchant from th' Exchange returns in Peace,

And the long Labours of the Toilette cease –
Belinda now, whom Thirst of Fame invites,
Burns to encounter two adventrous Knights,
At Ombre singly to decide their Doom;
And swells her Breast with Conquests yet to come.
Strait the three Bands prepare in Arms to join,
Each Band the number of the Sacred Nine.
Soon as she spreads her Hand, th' Aerial Guard
Descend, and sit on each important Card:
First Ariel perch'd upon a Matadore,
Then each, according to the Rank they bore;
For Sylphs, yet mindful of their ancient Race,
Are, as when Women, wondrous fond of Place.

Behold, four Kings in Majesty rever'd,
With hoary Whiskers and a forky Beard;
And four fair Queens whose hands sustain a Flow'r,
Th' expressive Emblem of their softer Pow'r;
For Knaves in Garbs succinct, a trusty Band,
Caps on their heads, and Halberds in their hand;
And Particolour'd Troops, a shining Train,
Draw forth to Combat on the Velvet Plain.

The skilful Nymph reviews her Force with Care;
Let Spades be Trumps! she said, and Trumps they were.

Now move to War her Sable Matadores,
In Show like Leaders of the swarthy Moors.
Spadillio first, unconquerable Lord!
Led off two captive Trumps, and swept the Board.
As many more Manillio forc'd to yield,

And march'd a Victor from the verdant Field.
Him Basto follow'd, but his Fate more hard
Gain'd but one Trump and one Plebeian Card.
With his broad Sabre next, a Chief in Years,
The hoary Majesty of Spades appears;
Puts forth one manly Leg, to sight reveal'd;
The rest his many-colour'd Robe conceal'd.
The Rebel-Knave, who dares his Prince engage,
Proves the just Victim of his Royal Rage.
Ev'n mighty Pam that Kings and Queens o'erthrew,
And mow'd down Armies in the Fights of Lu,
Sad Chance of War! now, destitute of Aid,
Falls undistinguish'd by the Victor Spade!

Thus far both Armies to Belinda yield;
Now to the Baron Fate inclines the Field,
His warlike Amazon her Host invades,
Th' Imperial Consort of the Crown of Spades.
The Club's black Tyrant first her victim dy'd,
Spite of his haughty Mien, and barb'rous Pride:
What boots the Regal Circle on his Head,
His Giant Limbs in State unwieldy spread?
That long behind he trails his pompous Robe,
And of all Monarchs only grasps the Globe?

The Baron now his Diamonds pours apace;
Th' embroider'd King who shows but half his Face,
And his refulgent Queen, with Pow'rs combin'd,
Of broken Troops an easie Conquest find.
Clubs, Diamonds, Hearts, in wild Disorder seen,

With Throngs promiscuous strow the level Green.
Thus when dispers'd a routed Army runs,
Of Asia's Troops, and Africk's Sable Sons,
With like Confusion different Nations fly,
Of various Habit and of various Dye,
The pierc'd Battalions dis-united fall,
In Heaps on Heaps; one Fate o'erwhelms them all.

The Knave of Diamonds tries his wily Arts,
And wins (oh shameful Chance!) the Queen of Hearts.
At this, the Blood the Virgin's Cheek forsook,
A livid Paleness spreads o'er all her Look;
She sees, and trembles at th' approaching Ill,
Just in the Jaws of Ruin, and Codille,
And now, (as oft in some distemper'd State)
On one nice Trick depends the gen'ral Fate.
An Ace of Hearts steps forth: The King unseen
Lurk'd in her Hand, and mourn'd his captive Queen.
He springs to Vengeance with an eager pace,
And falls like Thunder on the prostrate Ace.
The Nymph exulting fills with Shouts the Sky,
The Walls, the Woods, and long Canals reply.

Oh thoughtless Mortals! ever blind to Fate,
Too soon dejected, and too soon elate!
Sudden these Honours shall be snatch'd away,
And curs'd for ever this Victorious Day.

For lo! the Board with Cups and Spoons is crown'd,
The Berries crackle, and the Mill turns round.
On shining Altars of Japan they raise

The silver Lamp; the fiery Spirits blaze.
From silver Spouts the grateful Liquors glide,
While China's Earth receives the smoking Tyde.
At once they gratify their Scent and Taste,
And frequent Cups prolong the rich Repast.
Strait hover round the Fair her Airy Band;
Some, as she sip'd, the fuming Liquor fann'd,
Some o'er her Lap their careful Plumes display'd,
Trembling, and conscious of the rich Brocade.
Coffee, (which makes the Politician wise,
And see thro' all things with his half-shut Eyes)
Sent up in Vapours to the Baron's Brain
New Stratagems, the radiant Lock to gain.
Ah cease rash Youth! desist ere 'tis too late,
Fear the just Gods, and think of Scylla's Fate!
Chang'd to a Bird, and sent to flit in Air,
She dearly pays for Nisus' injur'd Hair!

But when to Mischief Mortals bend their Will,
How soon they find fit Instruments of Ill!
Just then, Clarissa drew with tempting Grace
A two-edg'd Weapon from her shining Case;
So Ladies in Romance assist their Knight,
Present the Spear; and arm him for the Fight.
He takes the Gift with rev'rence, and extends
The little Engine on his Fingers' Ends,
This just behind Belinda's Neck he spread,
As o'er the fragrant Steams she bends her Head:
Swift to the Lock a thousand Sprights repair,

A thousand Wings, by turns, blow back the Hair,
And thrice they twitch'd the Diamond in her Ear,
Thrice she look'd back, and thrice the Foe drew near.
Just in that instant, anxious Ariel sought
The close Recesses of the Virgin's Thought;
As on the Nosegay in her Breast reclin'd,
He watch'd th' Ideas rising in her Mind,
Sudden he view'd, in spite of all her Art,
An Earthly Lover lurking at her Heart.
Amaz'd, confus'd, he found his Pow'r expir'd,
Resign'd to Fate, and with a Sigh retir'd.

    The Peer now spreads the glitt'ring Forfex wide,
T'inclose the Lock; now joins it, to divide.
Ev'n then, before the fatal Engine clos'd,
A wretched Sylph too fondly interpos'd;
Fate urg'd the Sheers, and cut the Sylph in twain,
(But Airy Substance soon unites again)
The meeting Points the sacred Hair dissever
From the fair Head, for ever and for ever!

    Then flash'd the living Lightning from her Eyes,
And Screams of Horror rend th' affrighted Skies.
Not louder Shrieks to pitying Heav'n are cast,
When Husbands or when Lap-dogs breathe their last,
Or when rich China Vessels, fal'n from high,
In glittring Dust and painted Fragments lie!

    Let Wreaths of Triumph now my Temples twine,
(The Victor cry'd) the glorious Prize is mine!
While Fish in Streams, or Birds delight in air,

Or in a Coach and Six the British Fair,
As long as Atalantis shall be read,
Or the small Pillow grace a Lady's Bed,
While Visits shall be paid on solemn Days,
When numerous Wax-lights in bright Order blaze,
While Nymphs take Treats, or Assignations give,
So long my Honour, Name, and Praise shall live!

What Time wou'd spare, from Steel receives its date,
And Monuments, like Men, submit to Fate!
Steel cou'd the Labour of the Gods destroy,
And strike to Dust th' Imperial Tow'rs of Troy;
Steel cou'd the Works of mortal Pride confound,
And hew Triumphal Arches to the Ground.
What Wonder then, fair Nymph! thy Hairs shou'd feel
The conqu'ring Force of unresisted Steel?

CANTO IV

But anxious Cares the pensive Nymph opprest,
And secret Passions labour'd in her Breast.
Not youthful Kings in Battel seiz'd alive,
Not scornful Virgins who their Charms survive,
Not ardent Lovers robb'd of all their Bliss,
Not ancient Ladies when refus'd a Kiss,
Not Tyrants fierce that unrepenting die,
Not Cynthia when her Manteau's pinn'd awry,
E'er felt such Rage, Resentment and Despair,
As Thou, sad Virgin! for thy ravish'd Hair.

For, that sad moment, when the Sylphs withdrew, 23

And Ariel weeping from Belinda flew,
Umbriel, a dusky melancholy Spright,
As ever sully'd the fair face of Light,
Down to the Central Earth, his proper Scene,
Repair'd to search the gloomy Cave of Spleen.

Swift on his sooty Pinions flitts the Gnome,
And in Vapour reach'd the dismal Dome.
No cheerful Breeze this sullen Region knows,
The dreaded East is all the Wind that blows.
Here, in a Grotto, sheltred close from Air,
And screen'd in Shades from Day's detested Glare,
She sighs for ever on her pensive Bed,
Pain at her Side, and Megrim at her Head.

Two Handmaids wait the Throne: Alike in Place,
But diff'ring far in Figure and in Face.
Here stood Ill-nature like an ancient Maid,
Her wrinkled Form in Black and White array'd;
With store of Pray'rs, for Mornings, Nights, and Noons,
Her Hand is fill'd; her Bosom with Lampoons.

There Affectation with a sickly Mien
Shows in her Cheek the Roses of Eighteen,
Practis'd to Lisp, and hang the Head aside,
Faints into Airs, and languishes with Pride;
On the rich Quilt sinks with becoming Woe,
Wrapt in a Gown, for Sickness, and for Show.
The Fair-ones feel such Maladies as these,
When each new Night-Dress gives a new Disease.

A constant Vapour o'er the Palace flies;

Strange Phantoms rising as the Mists arise;
Dreadful, as Hermit's Dreams in haunted Shades,
Or bright as Visions of expiring Maids.
Now glaring Fiends, and Snakes on rolling Spires,
Pale Spectres, gaping Tombs, and Purple Fires:
Now Lakes of liquid Gold, Elysian Scenes,
And Crystal Domes, and Angels in Machines.

Unnumber'd Throngs on ev'ry side are seen
Of Bodies chang'd to various Forms by Spleen.
Here living Teapots stand, one Arm held out,
One bent; the Handle this, and that the Spout;
A Pipkin there like Homer's Tripod walks;
Here sighs a Jar, and there a Goose-pye talks;
Men prove with Child, as pow'rful Fancy works,
And Maids turn'd Bottels, call aloud for Corks.

Safe past the Gnome thro' this fantastick Band,
A Branch of healing Spleenwort in his hand.
Then thus addrest the Pow'r – Hail wayward Queen!
Who rule the Sex to Fifty from Fifteen,
Parent of Vapours and of Female Wit,
Who give th' Hysteric or Poetic Fit,
On various Tempers act by various ways,
Make some take Physick, others scribble Plays;
Who cause the Proud their Visits to delay,
And send the Godly in a Pett, to pray.
A Nymph there is, that all thy Pow'r disdains,
And thousands more in equal Mirth maintains
But oh! if e'er thy Gnome could spoil a Grace,

Or raise a Pimple on a beauteous Face,
Like Citron-Waters Matrons' Cheeks inflame,
Or change Complexion at a losing Game;
If e'er with airy Horns I planted Heads,
Or rumpled Petticoats, or tumbled Beds,
Or caus'd Suspicion when no Soul was rude,
Or discompos'd the Head-dress of a Prude,
Or e'er to costive Lap-Dog gave Disease,
Which not the Tears of brightest Eyes could ease:
Hear me, and touch Belinda with Chagrin;
That single Act gives half the World the Spleen.

   The Goddess with a discontented Air
Seems to reject him, tho' she grants his Pray'r.
A wondrous Bag with both her Hands she binds,
Like that where once Ulysses held the Winds;
There she collects the Force of Female Lungs,
Sighs, Sobs, and Passions, and the War of Tongues.
A Vial next she fills with fainting Fears,
Soft Sorrows, melting Griefs, and flowing Tears.
The Gnome rejoicing bears her Gifts away,
Spreads his black Wings, and slowly mounts to Day.

   Sunk in Thalestris's Arms the Nymph he found,
Her Eyes dejected and her Hair unbound.
Full o'er their Heads the swelling Bag he rent,
And all the Furies issued at the Vent.
Belinda burns with more than mortal Ire,
And fierce Thalestris fans the rising Fire.
O wretched Maid! she spread her Hands, and cry'd,

(While Hampton's Ecchos, wretched Maid! reply'd)
Was it for this you took such constant Care
The Bodkin, Comb, and Essence to prepare;
For this your Locks in Paper-Durance bound,
For this with tort'ring Irons wreath'd around?
For this with Fillets strain'd your tender Head,
And bravely bore the double Loads of Lead?
Gods! shall the Ravisher display your Hair,
While the Fops envy, and the Ladies stare!
Honour forbid! at whose unrival'd Shrine
Ease, Pleasure, Virtue, All, our Sex resign.
Methinks already I your Tears survey,
Already hear the horrid things they say,
Already see you a degraded Toast,
And all your Honour in a Whisper lost!
How shall I, then, your helpless Fame defend?
'Twill then be Infamy to seem your Friend!
And shall this Prize, th' inestimable Prize,
Expos'd thro' Crystal to the gazing Eyes,
And heighten'd by the Diamond's circling Rays,
On that Rapacious Hand for ever blaze?
Sooner shall Grass in Hide-Park Circus grow,
And Wits take Lodgings in the Sound of Bow;
Sooner let Earth, Air, Sea, to Chaos fall,
Men, Monkies, Lap-dogs, Parrots, perish all!
   She said; then raging to Sir Plume repairs,
And bids her Beau demand the precious Hairs:
(Sir Plume, of Amber Snuff-box justly vain,

And the nice Conduct of a clouded Cane)
With earnest Eyes, and round unthinking Face,
He first the Snuff-box open'd, then the Case,
And thus broke out – 'My Lord, why, what the Devil?
Z – ds! damn the Lock! 'fore God, you must be civil!
Plague on't! 'tis past a Jest – nay prithee, Pox!
Give her the Hair' – he spoke, and rapp'd his Box.

It grieves me much (reply'd the Peer again)
Who speaks so well shou'd ever speak in vain.
But by this Lock, this sacred Lock I swear,
(Which never more shall join its parted Hair,
Which never more its Honours shall renew,
Clipt from the lovely Head where late it grew)
That while my Nostrils draw the vital Air,
This Hand, which won it, shall for ever wear.
He spoke, and speaking, in proud Triumph spread
The long-contended Honours of her Head.

But Umbriel, hateful Gnome! forbears not so;
He breaks the Vial whence the Sorrows flow.
Then see! the Nymph in beauteous Grief appears,
Her Eyes half-languishing, half-drown'd in Tears;
On her heav'd Bosom hung her drooping Head,
Which, with a Sigh, she rais'd; and thus she said.

For ever curs'd be this detested Day,
Which snatch'd my best, my fav'rite Curl away!
Happy! ah ten times happy, had I been,
If Hampton-Court these Eyes had never seen!
Yet am not I the first mistaken Maid,

By Love of Courts to num'rous Ills betray'd.
Oh had I rather un-admir'd remain'd
In some lone Isle, or distant Northern land;
Where the gilt Chariot never marks the Way,
Where none learn Ombre, none e'er taste Bohea!
There kept my Charms conceal'd from mortal Eye,
Like Roses that in Desarts bloom and die.
What mov'd my Mind with youthful Lords to rome?
O had I stay'd, and said my Pray'rs at home!
'Twas this, the Morning Omens seem'd to tell;
Thrice from my trembling hand the Patch-box fell;
The tott'ring China shook without a Wind,
Nay, Poll sate mute, and Shock was most Unkind!
A Sylph too warn'd me of the Threats of Fate,
In mystic Visions, now believ'd too late!
See the poor Remnants of these slightest Hairs!
My hands shall rend what ev'n thy Rapine spares:
These, in two sable Ringlets taught to break,
Once gave new Beauties to the snowie Neck.
The Sister-Lock now sits uncouth, alone,
And in its Fellow's Fate foresees its own;
Uncurl'd it hangs, the fatal Sheers demands;
And tempts once more thy sacrilegious Hands.
Oh hadst thou, Cruel! been content to seize
Hairs less in sight, or any Hairs but these!

She said: the pitying Audience melt in Tears,
But Fate and Jove had stopp'd the Baron's Ears.
In vain Thalestris with Reproach assails,
For who can move when fair Belinda fails?
Not half so fixt the Trojan cou'd remain,
While Anna begg'd and Dido rag'd in vain.
Then grave Clarissa graceful wav'd her Fan;
Silence ensu'd, and thus the Nymph began.

Say, why are Beauties prais'd and honour'd most,
The wise Man's Passion, and the vain Man's Toast?
Why deck'd with all that Land and Sea afford,
Why Angels call'd, and Angel-like ador'd?
Why round our Coaches crowd the white-glov'd Beaus,
Why bows the Side-box from its inmost Rows?
How vain are all these Glories, all our Pains,
Unless good Sense preserve what Beauty gains:
That Men may say, when we the Front-box grace,
Behold the first in Virtue, as in Face!
Oh! if to dance all Night, and dress all Day,
Charm'd the Small pox, or chas'd old Age away;
Who would not scorn what Huswife's Cares produce,
Or who would learn one earthly Thing of Use?
To patch, nay ogle, might become a Saint,
Nor could it sure be such a Sin to paint.
But since, alas! frail Beauty must decay,
Curl'd or uncurl'd, since Locks will turn to grey,
Since painted, or not painted, all shall fade,

And she who scorns a Man, must die a Maid;
What then remains, but well our Pow'r to use,
And keep good Humour still whate'er we lose?
And trust me, Dear! good Humour can prevail,
When Airs, and Flights, and Screams, and Scolding fail.
Beauties in vain their pretty Eyes may roll;
Charms strike the Sight, but Merit wins the Soul.

So spoke the Dame, but no Applause ensu'd;
Belinda frown'd, Thalestris call'd her Prude.
To Arms, to Arms! the fierce Virago cries,
And swift as Lightning to the Combate flies.
All side in Parties, and begin th' Attack;
Fans clap, Silks russle, and tough Whalebones crack;
Heroes' and Heroins' Shouts confus'dly rise,
And base, and treble Voices strike the Skies.
No common Weapons in their Hands are found,
Like Gods they fight, nor dread a mortal Wound.

So when bold Homer makes the Gods engage,
And heav'nly Breasts with human Passions rage;
'Gainst Pallas, Mars; Latona, Hermes arms;
And all Olympus rings with loud Alarms.
Jove's Thunder roars, Heav'n trembles all around;
Blue Neptune storms, the bellowing Deeps resound;
Earth shakes her nodding Tow'rs, the Ground gives way;
And the pale Ghosts start at the Flash of Day!

Triumphant Umbriel on a Sconce's Height
Clapt his glad Wings, and sate to view the Fight:
Propt on their Bodkin Spears, the Sprights survey

The growing Combat, or assist the Fray.

While thro' the Press enrag'd Thalestris flies,
And scatters Deaths around from both her Eyes,
A Beau and Witling perish'd in the Throng,
One dy'd in Metaphor, and one in Song.
O cruel Nymph! a living Death I bear,
Cry'd Dapperwit, and sunk beside his Chair.
A mournful Glance Sir Fopling upwards cast,
Those Eyes are made so killing – was his last:
Thus on Meander's flow'ry Margin lies
Th' expiring Swan, and as he sings he dies.

When bold Sir Plume had drawn Clarissa down,
Chloe stept in, and kill'd him with a Frown;
She smil'd to see the doughty Hero slain,
But at her Smile, the Beau reviv'd again.

Now Jove suspends his golden Scales in Air,
Weighs the Men's Wits against the Lady's Hair;
The doubtful Beam long nods from side to side;
At length the Wits mount up, the Hairs subside.

See fierce Belinda on the Baron flies,
With more than usual Lightning in her Eyes;
Nor fear'd the Chief th' unequal Fight to try,
Who sought no more than on his Foe to die.
But this bold Lord, with manly Strength indu'd,
She with one Finger and a Thumb subdu'd:
Just where the Breadth of Life his Nostrils drew,
A Charge of Snuff the wily Virgin threw;
The Gnomes direct, to ev'ry Atome just,

The pungent Grains of titillating Dust.
Sudden, with starting Tears each Eye o'erflows,
And the high Dome re-ecchoes to his Nose.

Now meet thy Fate, incens'd Belinda cry'd,
And drew a deadly Bodkin from her Side.
(The same, his ancient Personage to deck,
Her great great Grandsire wore about his Neck
In three Seal-Ring; which after, melted down,
Form'd a vast Buckle for his Widow's Gown:
Her infant Grandame's Whistle next it grew,
The Bells she gingled, and the Whistle blew;
Then in a Bodkin grac'd her Mother's Hairs,
Which long she wore, and now Belinda wears.)

Boast not my Fall (he cry'd) insulting Foe!
Thou by some other shalt be laid as low.
Nor think, to die dejects my lofty Mind;
All that I dread, is leaving you behind!
Rather than so, ah let me still survive,
And burn in Cupid's Flames, – but burn alive.

Restore the Lock! she cries; and all around
Restore the Lock! the vaulted Roofs rebound.
Not fierce Othello in so loud a Strain
Roar'd for the Handkerchief that caus'd his Pain.
But see how oft Ambitious Aims are cross'd,
And Chiefs contend 'till all the Prize is lost!
The Lock, obtain'd with Guilt, and kept with Pain,
In ev'ry place is sought, but sought in vain:
With such a Prize no Mortal must be blest,

So Heav'n decrees! with Heav'n who can contest?
　Some thought it mounted to the Lunar Sphere,
Since all things lost on Earth, are treasur'd there.
There Heroes' Wits are kept in pondrous Vases,
And Beaus' in Snuff-boxes and Tweezer-Cases.
There broken Vows, and Death-bed Alms are found,
And Lovers' Hearts with Ends of Riband bound;
The Courtier's Promises, and Sick Man's Pray'rs,
The Smiles of Harlots, and the Tears of Heirs,
Cages for Gnats, and Chains to Yoak a Flea;
Dry'd Butterflies, and Tomes of Casuistry.
　But trust the Muse – she saw it upward rise,
Tho' mark'd by none but quick Poetic Eyes:
(So Rome's great Founder to the Heav'ns withdrew,
To Proculus alone confess'd in view.)
A sudden Star, it shot thro' liquid Air,
And drew behind a radiant Trail of Hair.
Not Berenice's Locks first rose so bright,
The heav'ns bespangling with dishevel'd Light.
The Sylphs behold it kindling as it flies,
And pleas'd pursue its Progress thro' the Skies.
　This the Beau-monde shall from the Mall survey,
And hail with Musick its propitious Ray.
This, the blest Lover shall for Venus take,
And sent up Vows from Rosamonda's Lake.
This Partridge soon shall view in cloudless Skies,
When next he looks thro' Galilæo's Eyes;
And hence th' Egregious Wizard shall foredoom

The Fate of Louis, and the Fall of Rome.
  Then cease, bright Nymph! to mourn thy ravish'd Hair
Which adds new Glory to the shining Sphere!
Not all the Tresses that fair Head can boast
Shall draw such Envy as the Lock you lost.
For, after all the Murders of your Eye,
When, after Millions slain, your self shall die;
When those fair Suns shall sett, as sett they must,
And all those Tresses shall be laid in Dust;
This Lock, the Muse shall consecrate to Fame,
And mid'st the Stars inscribe Belinda's Name!

Eloisa to Abelard

In these deep solitudes and awful cells,
Where heav'nly-pensive, contemplation dwells,
And ever-musing melancholy reigns;
What means this tumult in a Vestal's veins?
Why rove my thoughts beyond this last retreat?
Why feels my heart its long-forgotten heat?
Yet, yet I love! – From Abelard it came,
And Eloisa yet must kiss the name.
  Dear fatal name! rest ever unreveal'd,
Nor pass these lips in holy silence seal'd.
Hide it, my heart, within that close disguise,
Where, mix'd with God's, his lov'd Idea lies.
Oh write it not, my hand – The name appears

Already written – wash it out, my tears!
In vain lost Eloisa weeps and prays,
Her heart still dictates, and her hand obeys.
    Relentless walls! whose darksom round contains
Repentant sighs, and voluntary pains;
Ye rugged rocks! which holy knees have worn;
Ye grots and caverns shagg'd with horrid thorn!
Shrines! where their vigils pale-ey'd virgins keep,
And pitying saints, whose statues learn to weep!
Tho' cold like you, unmov'd, and silent grown,
I have not yet forgot my self to stone.
All is not Heav'n's while Abelard has part,
Still rebel nature holds out half my heart;
Nor pray'rs nor fast its stubborn pulse restrain,
Nor tears, for ages, taught to flow in vain.
    Soon as thy letters trembling I unclose,
That well-known name awakens all my woes.
Oh name for ever sad! for ever dear!
Still breath'd in sighs, still usher'd with a tear.
I tremble too where-e'er my own I find,
Some dire misfortune follows close behind.
Line after line my gushing eyes o'erflow,
Led thro' a sad variety of woe:
Now warm in love, now with'ring in thy bloom,
Lost in a convent's solitary gloom!
There stern religion quench'd th' unwilling flame,
There dy'd the best of passions, Love and Fame.
       Yet write, or write me all, that I may join

Griefs to thy griefs, and eccho sighs to thine.
Nor foes nor fortune take this pow'r away.
And is my Abelard less kind than they?
Tears still are mine, and those I need not spare,
Love but demands what else were shed in pray'r;
No happier task these faded eyes pursue,
To read and weep is all they now can do.

Then share thy pain, allow that sad relief;
Ah more than share it! give me all thy grief.
Heav'n first taught letters for some wretch'd aid,
Some banish'd lover, or some captive maid;
They live, they speak, they breathe what love inspires,
Warm from the soul, and faithful to its fires,
The virgin's wish without her fears impart,
Excuse the blush, and pour out all the heart,
Speed the soft intercourse from soul to soul,
And waft a sigh from Indus to the Pole.

Thou know'st how guiltless first I met thy flame,
When Love approach'd me under Friendship's name;
My fancy form'd thee of Angelick kind,
Some emanation of th' all-beauteous Mind.
Those smiling eyes, attemp'ring ev'ry ray,
Shone sweetly lambent with celestial day:
Guiltless I gaz'd; heav'n listen'd while you sung;
And truths divine came mended from that tongue.
From lips like those what precept fail'd to move?
Too soon they taught me 'twas no sin to love.
Back thro' the paths of pleasing sense I ran,

Nor wish'd an Angel whom I lov'd a Man.
Dim and remote the joys of saints I see,
Nor envy them, that heav'n I lose for thee.
    How oft', when press'd to marriage, have I said,
Curse on all laws but those which love has made!
Love, free as air, at sight of human ties,
Spreads his light wings, and in a moment flies.
Let wealth, let honour, wait the wedded dame,
August her deed, and sacred be her fame;
Before true passion all those views remove,
Fame, wealth, and honour! what are you to Love?
The jealous God, when we profane his fires,
Those restless passions in revenge inspires;
And bids them make mistaken mortals groan,
Who seek in love for ought but love alone.
Should at my feet the world's great master fall,
Himself, his throne, his world, I'd scorn 'em all:
Not Cæsar's empress wou'd I deign to prove;
No, make me mistress to the man I love;
If there be yet another name more free,
More fond than mistress, make me that to thee!
Oh happy state! when souls each other draw,
When love is liberty, and nature, law:
All then is full, possessing, and possest,
No craving Void left aking in the breast:
Ev'n thought meets thought ere from the lips it part,
And each warm wish springs mutual from the heart.
This sure is bliss (if bliss on earth there be)

And once the lot of Abelard and me.
    Alas how chang'd! what sudden horrors rise!
A naked Lover bound and bleeding lies!
Where, where was Eloise? her voice, her hand,
Her ponyard, had oppos'd the dire command.
Barbarian stay! that bloody stroke restrain;
The crime was common, common be the pain.
I can no more; by shame, by rage supprest,
Let tears, and burning blushes speak the rest.
    Canst thou forget that sad, that solemn day,
When victims at yon' altar's foot we lay?
Canst thou forget what tears that moment fell,
When, warm in youth, I bade the world farewell?
As with cold lips I kiss'd the sacred veil,
The shrines all trembled, and the lamps grew gale:
Heav'n scarce believ'd the conquest it survey'd,
And Saints with wonder heard the vows I made.
Yet then, to those dread altars as I drew,
Not on the Cross my eyes were fix'd, but you;
Not grave, or zeal, love only was my call,
And if I lose thy love, I lose my all.
Come! with thy looks, thy words, relieve my woe;
Those still at least are left thee to bestow.
Still on that breast enamour'd let me lie,
Still drink delicious poison from thy eye,
Pant on thy lip, and to thy heart be prest;
Give all thou canst – and let me dream the rest.
Ah no! instruct me other joys to prize,

With other beauties charm my partial eyes,
Full in my view set all the bright abode,
And make my soul quit Abelard for God.

Ah think at least thy flock deserves thy care,
Plants of thy hand, and children of thy pray'r.
From the false world in early youth they fled,
By thee to mountains, wilds, and deserts led.
You rais'd these hallow'd walls; the desert smil'd,
And Paradise was open'd in the Wild.
No weeping orphan saw his father's stores
Our shrines irradiate, or emblaze the floors;
No silver saints, by dying misers giv'n,
Here brib'd the rage of ill-requited heav'n:
But such plain roofs as piety could raise,
And only vocal with the Maker's praise.
In these lone walls (their day's eternal bound)
These moss-grown domes with spiry turrets crown'd,
Where awful arches made a noon-day night,
And the dim windows shed a solemn light;
Thy eyes diffus'd a reconciling ray,
And gleams of glory brighten'd all the day,
But now no face divine contentment wears,
'Tis all blank sadness, or continual tears.
See how the force of others' pray'rs I try,
(Oh pious fraud of am'rous charity!)
But why should I on others' pray'rs depend?
Come thou, father, brother, husband, friend!
Ah let thy handmaid, sister, daughter, move,

And, all those tender names in one, thy love!
The darksom pines that o'er yon' rocks reclin'd
Wave high, and murmur to the hollow wind,
The wandring streams that shine between the hills,
The grots that eccho to the tinkling rills,
The dying gales that pant upon the trees,
The lakes that quiver to the curling breeze;
No more these scenes my meditation aid,
Or lull to rest the visionary maid:
But o'er the twilight groves, and dusky caves,
Long-sounding isles, and intermingled graves,
Black Melancholy sits, and round her throws
A death-like silence, and a dread repose:
Her gloomy presence saddens all the scene,
Shades ev'ry flow'r, and darkens ev'ry green,
Deepens the murmur of the falling floods,
And breathes a browner horror on the woods.

   Yet here for ever, ever must I stay;
Sad proof how well a lover can obey!
Death, only death, can break the lasting chain;
And here ev'n then, shall my cold dust remain,
Here all its frailties, all its flames resign,
And wait, till 'tis no sin to mix with thine.

   Ah wretch! believ'd the spouse of God in vain,
Confess'd within the slave of love and man.
Assist me heav'n! but whence arose that pray'r?
Sprung it from piety, or from despair?
Ev'n here, where frozen chastity retires,

Love finds an altar for forbidden fires.
I ought to grieve, but cannot what I ought;
I mourn the lover, not lament the fault;
I view my crime, but kindle at the view,
Repent old pleasures, and sollicit new:
Now turn'd to heav'n, I weep my past offence,
Now think of thee, and curse my innocence.
Of all affliction taught a lover yet,
'Tis sure the hardest science to forget!
How shall I lose the sin, yet keep the sense,
And love th' offender, yet detest th' offence?
How the dear object from the crime remove,
Or how distinguish penitence from love?
Unequal task! a passion to resign,
For hearts so touch'd, so pierc'd, so lost as mine.
Ere such a soul regains its peaceful state,
How often must it love, how often hate!
How often, hope, despair, resent, regret,
Conceal, disdain – do all things but forget.
But let heav'n seize it, all at once 'tis fir'd,
Not touch'd, but rapt, not waken'd, but inspir'd!
Oh come! oh teach me nature to subdue,
Renounce my love, my life, my self – and you.
Fill my fond heart with God alone, for he
Alone can rival, can succeed to thee.
    How happy is the blameless Vestal's lot!
The world forgetting, by the world forgot.
Eternal sun-shine of the spotless mind!

Each pray'r accepted, and each wish resign'd;
Labour and rest, that equal periods keep;
'Obedient slumbers that can wake and weep';
Desires compos'd, affections ever ev'n, ·
Tears that delight, and sighs that waft to heav'n.
Grace shines around her with serenest beams,
And whisp'ring Angels prompt her golden dreams.
For her th' unfading rose of Eden blooms,
And wings of Seraphs shed divine perfumes;
For her the Spouse prepares the bridal ring,
For her white virgins Hymenæals sing;
To sounds of heav'nly harps, she dies away,
And melts in visions of eternal day.

Far other dreams my erring soul employ,
Far other raptures, of unholy joy:
When at the close of each sad, sorrowing day,
Fancy restores what vengeance snatch'd away,
Then conscience sleeps, and leaving nature free,
All my loose soul unbounded springs to thee.
O curst, dear horrors of all-conscious night!
How flowing guilt exalts the keen delight!
Provoking Dæmons all restraint remove,
And stir within me ev'ry source of love,
I hear thee, view thee, gaze o'er all thy charms,
And round thy phantom glue my clasping arms.
I wake – no more I hear, no more I view,
The phantom flies me, as unkind as you,
I call aloud; it hears not what I say;

43

I stretch my empty arms; it glides away:
To dream once more I close my willing eyes;
Ye soft illusions, dear deceits, arise!
Alas no more! – methinks we wandring go
Thro' dreary wastes, and weep each other's woe;
Where round some mould'ring tow'r pale ivy creeps,
And low-brow'd rocks hang nodding o'er the deeps.
Sudden you mount! you becken from the skies;
Clouds interpose, waves roar, and winds arise.
I shriek, start up, the same sad prospect find,
And wake to all the griefs I left behind.

For thee the fates, severally kind, ordain
A cool suspense from pleasure and from pain;
Thy life a long, dead calm of fix'd repose;
No pulse that riots, and no blood that glows.
Still as the sea, ere winds were taught to blow,
Or moving spirit bade the waters flow;
Soft as the slumbers of a saint forgiv'n,
And mild as opening gleams of promis'd heav'n.

Come Abelard! for what hast thou to dread?
The torch of Venus burns not for the dead;
Nature stands check'd; Religion disapproves;
Ev'n thou art cold – yet Eloisa loves.
Ah hopeless, lasting flames! like those that burn
To light the dead, and warm th' unfruitful urn.

What scenes appear where-e'er I turn my view!
The dear Ideas, where I fly, pursue,
Rise in the grove, before the altar rise,

Stain all my soul, and wanton in my eyes!
I waste the Matin lamp in sighs for thee,
Thy image steals between my God and me,
Thy voice I seem in ev'ry hymn to hear,
With ev'ry bead I drop too soft a tear.
When from the Censer clouds of fragrance roll,
And swelling organs lift the rising soul;
One thought of thee puts all the pomp to flight,
Priests, Tapers, Temples, swim before my sight:
In seas of flame my plunging soul is drown'd,
While Altars blaze, and Angels tremble round.

   While prostrate here in humble grief I lie,
Kind, virtuous drops just gath'ring in my eye,
While praying, trembling, in the dust I roll,
And dawning grace is opening on my soul:
Come, thou dar'st, all charming as thou art!
Oppose thy self to heav'n; dispute my heart;
Come, with one glance of those deluding eyes,
Blot out each bright Idea of the skies.
Take back that grace, those sorrows, and those tears,
Take back my fruitless penitence and pray'rs,
Snatch me, just mounting, from the blest abode,
Assist the Fiends and tear me from my God!

   No, fly me, fly me! far as Pole from Pole;
Rise Alps between us! and whole oceans roll!
Ah come not, write not, think not once of me,
Nor share one pang of all I felt for thee.
Thy oaths I quit, thy memory resign,

Forget, renounce me, hate whate'er was mine.
Fair eyes, and tempting looks (which yet I view!)
Long lov'd, ador'd ideas! all adieu!
O grace serene! oh virtue heav'nly fair!
Divine oblivion of low-thoughted care!
Fresh blooming hope, gay daughter of the sky!
And faith, our early immortality!
Enter each mild, each amicable guest;
Receive, and wrap me in eternal rest!

   See in her Cell sad Eloisa spread,
Propt on some tomb, a neighbour of the dead!
In each low wind methinks a Spirit calls,
And more than Echoes talk along the walls.
Here, as I watch'd the dying lamps around,
From yonder shrine I heard a hollow sound.
Come, sister come! (it said, or seem'd to say)
Thy place is here, sad sister come away!
Once like thy self, I trembled, wept, and pray'd,
Love's victim then, tho' now a sainted maid:
But all is calm in this eternal sleep;
Here grief forgets to groan, and love to weep,
Ev'n superstition loses ev'ry fear:
For God, not man, absolves our frailties here.

   I come, I come! prepare your roseate bow'rs,
Celestial palms, and ever-blooming flow'rs.
Thither, where sinners may have rest, I go,
Where flames refin'd in breasts seraphic glow.
Thou, Abelard! the last sad office pay,

And smooth my passage to the realms of day:
See my lips tremble, and my eye-balls roll,
Suck my last breath, and catch my flying soul!
Ah no – in sacred vestments may'st thou stand,
The hallow'd taper trembling in thy hand,
Present the Cross before my lifted eye,
Teach me at once, and learn of me to die.
Ah then, thy once-lov'd Eloisa see!
It will be then no crime to gaze on me.
See from my cheek the transient roses fly!
See the last sparkle languish in my eye!
Till ev'ry motion, pulse, and breath, be o'er;
And ev'n my Abelard be lov'd no more.
O death all-eloquent! you only prove
What dust we doat on, when 'tis man we love.

Then too, when fate shall thy fair frame destroy,
(That cause of all my guilt, and all my joy)
In trance extatic may thy pangs be drown'd,
Bright clouds descend, and Angels watch thee round,
From opening skies may streaming glories shine,
And Saints embrace thee with a love like mine.

May one kind grave unite each hapless name,
And graft my love immortal on thy fame.
Then, ages hence, when all my woes are o'er,
When this rebellious heart shall beat no more;
If ever chance two wandring lovers brings
To Paraclete's white walls, and silver springs,
O'er the pale marble shall they join their heads,

And drink the falling tears each other sheds,
Then sadly say, with mutual pity mov'd,
Oh may we never love as these have lov'd!
From the full quire when loud Hosanna's rise,
And swell the pomp of dreadful sacrifice,
Amid that scene, if some relenting eye
Glance on the stone where our cold reliques lie,
Devotion's self shall steal a thought from heav'n,
One human tear shall drop, and be forgiv'n.
And sure if fate some future Bard shall join
In sad similitude of griefs to mine,
Condemn'd whole years in absence to deplore,
And image charms he must behold no more,
Such if there be, who loves so long, so well;
Let him our sad, our tender story tell;
The well-sung woes will sooth my pensive ghost;
He best can paint 'em, who shall feel 'em most.

from The Dunciad

In vain, in vain, – the all-composing Hour
Resistless falls: the Muse obeys the Pow'r.
She comes! she comes! the sable Throne behold
Of Night Primeval, and of Chaos old!
Before her, Fancy's gilded clouds decay,
And all it varying Rain-bows die away.
Wit shoots in vain in momentary fires,

The meteor drops, and in a flash expires.
As one by one, at dread Medea's strain,
The sick'ning stars fade off th' ethereal plain;
As Argus' eyes, by Hermes' wand opprest,
Clos'd one by one to everlasting rest;
Thus at her felt approach, and secret might,
Art after Art goes out, and all is Night.
See skulking Truth to her old cavern fled,
Mountains of Casuistry heap'd o'er her head!
Philosophy, that lean'd on Heav'n before,
Shrinks to her second cause, and is no more.
Physic of Metaphysic begs defence,
And Metaphysic calls for aid on Sense!
See Mystery to Mathematics fly!
In vain! they gaze, turn giddy, rave, and die.
Religion blushing veils her sacred fires,
And unawares Morality expires.
Nor public Flame, nor private, dares to shine;
Nor human Spark is left, nor Glimpse divine!
Lo! thy dread Empire, CHAOS! is restor'd;
Light dies before thy uncreating word:
They hand, great Anarch! lets the curtain fall;
And universal Darkness buries All.

from An Essay on Man

II. Hope Eternal

Heav'n from all creatures hides the book of Fate,
All but the page prescrib'd, their present state:
From brutes what men, from men what spirits know:
Or who could suffer Being here below?
The lamb thy riot dooms to bleed to-day,
Had he thy Reason, would he skip and play?
Pleas'd to the last, he crops the flow'ry food,
And licks the hand just rais'd to shed his blood.
Oh blindness to the future! kindly giv'n,
That each may fill the circle mark'd by Heav'n:
Who sees with equal eye, as God, of all,
A hero perish, or a sparrow fall,
Atoms or systems into ruin hurl'd,
And now a bubble burst, and now a world.

   Hope humbly then; with trembling pinions soar;
Wait the great teacher Death; and God adore.
What future bliss, he gives not thee to know,
But gives that Hope to be thy blessing now.
Hope springs eternal in the human breast:
Man never Is, but always To be blest:
The soul uneasy, and confin'd from home,
Rests and expatiates in a life to come.

   Lo, the poor Indian! whose untutor'd mind
Sees God in clouds, or hears him in the wind;

His soul, proud Science never taught to stray
Far as the solar walk, or milky way;
Yet simple Nature to his hope has giv'n,
Behind the cloud-topt hill, an humbler heav'n;
Some safer world in depth of woods embrac'd,
Some happier island in the wat'ry waste,
Where slaves once more their native land behold,
No fiends torment, no Christians thirst for gold.
To Be, contents his natural desire,
He asks no Angel's wing, no Seraph's fire;
But thinks, admitted to that equal sky,
His faithful dog shall bear him company.

from Moral Essays

EPISTLE II: of the Characters of Women

Nothing so true as what you once let fall,
'Most Women have no Characters at all'.
Matter too soft a lasting mark to bear,
And best distinguish'd by black, brown, or fair.
   How many pictures of one Nymph we view,
All how unlike each other, all how true!
Arcadia's Countess, here, in ermin'd pride,
Is there, Pastora by a fountain side:
Here Fannia, leering on her own good man,
Is there, a naked Leda with a Swan.

Let then the Fair one beautifully cry,
In Magdalen's house hair and lifted eye,
Or drest in smiles of sweet Cecilia shine,
With simp'ring Angels, Palms, and Harps divine;
Whether the Charmer sinner it, or saint it,
If Folly grows romantic, I must paint it.

Come then, the colours and the ground prepare!
Dip in the Rainbow, trick her off in Air,
Chuse a firm Cloud, before it fall, and in it
Catch, ere she change, the Cynthia of this minute.

Rufa, whose eye quick-glancing o'er the Park,
Attracts each light gay meteor of a Spark,
Agrees as ill with Rufa studying Locke,
As Sappho's diamonds with her dirty smock,
Or Sappho at her toilet's greasy task,
With Sappho fragrant at an ev'ning Mask:
So morning Insects that in muck begun,
Shine, buzz, and fly-blow in the setting-sun.

How soft is Silia! fearful to offend,
The Frail one's advocate, the Weak one's friend:
To her, Calista prov'd her conduct nice,
And good Simplicius asks of her advice.
Sudden, she storms! she raves! You tip the wink,
But spare your censure; Silia does not drink.
All eyes may see from what the change arose,
All eyes may see – a Pimple on her nose.

Papillia, wedded to her doating spark,
Sighs for the shades – 'How charming is a Park!'

A Park is purchas'd, but the Fair he sees
All bath'd in tears – 'Oh odious, odious Trees!'
    Ladies, like variegated Tulips, show,
'Tis to their Changes that their charms we owe;
Their happy Spots the nice admirer take,
Fine by defect, and delicately weak.
'Twas thus Calypso once each heart alarm'd;
Aw'd without Virtue, without Beauty charm'd;
Her Tongue bewitch'd as odly as her Eyes,
Less Wit than Mimic, more a Wit than wise:
Strange graces still, and stranger flights she had,
Was just not ugly, and was just not mad;
Yet ne'er so sure our passion to create,
As when she touch'd the brink of all we hate.
    Narcissa's nature, tolerably mild,
To make a wash, would hardly stew a child,
Has ev'n been prov'd to grant a Lover's pray'r,
And paid a Tradesman once to make him stare,
Gave alms at Easter, in a Christian trim,
And made a Widow happy, for a whim.
Why then declare Good-nature is her scorn,
When 'tis by that alone she can be born?
Why pique all mortals, yet affect a name?
A fool to Pleasure, and a slave to Fame:
Now deep in Taylor and the Book of Martyrs,
Now drinking citron with his Grace and Chartres.
Now Conscience chills her, and now Passion burns;
And Atheism and Religion take their turns;

53

A very Heathen in the carnal part,
Yet still a sad, good Christian at her heart.

    See Sin in State, majestically drunk,
Proud as a Peeress, prouder as a Punk;
Chaste to her Husband, frank to all beside,
A teeming Mistress, but a barren Bride.
When then? let Blood and Body bear the fault,
Her Head's untouch'd, that noble Seat of Thought:
Such this day's doctrine – in another fit
She sins with Poets thro' pure Love of Wit.
What has not fir'd her bosom or her brain?
Cæsar and Tall-boy, Charles and Charlema'ne.
As Helluo, late Dictator of the Feast,
The Nose of Hautgout, and the Tip of Taste,
Critick'd your wine, and analyz'd your meat,
Yet on plain Pudding deign'd at-home to eat;
So Philomedé, lect'ring all mankind
On the soft Passion, and the Taste refin'd,
Th' Address, the Delicacy – stoops at once,
And makes her hearty meal upon a Dunce.

    Flavia's a Wit, has too much sense to Pray,
To Toast our wants and wishes, is her way;
Nor asks of God, but of her Stars to give
The mighty blessing, 'while we live, to live.'
Then all for Death, that Opiate of the soul!
Lucretia's dagger, Rosamonda's bowl.
Say, what can cause such impotence of mind?
A Spark too fickle, or a Spouse too kind.

Wise Wretch! with Pleasures too refin'd to please,
With too much Spirit to be e'er at ease,
With too much Quickness ever to be taught,
With too much Thinking to have common Thought:
Who purchase Pain with all that Joy can give,
And die of nothing but a Rage to live.

Turn then from Wits; and look on Simo's Mate,
No Ass so meek, no Ass so obstinate:
Or her, that owns her Faults, but never mends,
Because she's honest, and the best of Friends:
Or her, whose life the Church and Scandal share,
For ever in a Passion, or a Pray'r:
Or her, who laughs at Hell, but (like her Grace)
Cries, 'Ah! how charming if there's no such place!'
Or who in sweet vicissitude appears
Of Mirth and Opium, Ratafie and Tears,
The daily Anodyne, and nightly Draught,
To kill those foes to Fair ones, Time and Thought.
Woman and Fool are two hard things to hit,
For true No-meaning puzzles more than Wit.

But what are these to great Atossa's mind?

A Note on Alexander Pope

Alexander Pope (1688–1744), English poet, born in London. His parents were Roman Catholic and Pope received a somewhat desultory education at various Roman Catholic schools, but after the age of 12, when he had a severe illness which left him crippled, he was practically self-educated. Though never a profound or accurate scholar, he had a good knowledge of Latin and a working acquaintance with Greek. By 1704 he had written a good deal of verse, which attracted the attention of Wycherley, who introduced him to other men of letters.

In 1709 his *Pastorals*, written, according to his own account, at the age of 16, were published in Tonson's *Miscellany*, and two years later the *Essay on Criticism*, a neat and concise statement of neo-classical principles, appeared and was praised by Addison. The mock-heroic *Rape of the Lock*, published in 1714, then placed his reputation on a sure foundation. His industry was untiring, and his literary output almost continuous until his death. In 1713 *Windsor Forest*, a description of natural surroundings which incorporates observations on society and history, and *The Temple of Fame* appeared. *Windsor Forest* won for Pope the friendship of Swift. In 1715 the translation of the *Iliad* was begun, and published at intervals until 1720. It was enormously popular, and brought the poet £5000. The *Odyssey* followed (1725–26), although with this he had the assistance of Broome and Fenton, who caught his style exactly. It also was very popular, and increased his gains to about £8000, which placed him in a position of independence. While translating these poems, Pope moved to Chiswick, where he lived from 1716 to 1718, and where he issued in 1717 a collected edition of his works, including the 'Elegy on the Death of an Unfortunate Lady' and the *Epistle of Eloisa to Abelard*.

In 1718, his father having died, he moved with his mother to his famous villa at Twickenham; the setting out of the grounds here became one of his chief interests and here also he received his friends, who included the most distinguished men of letters, wits, statesmen, and beauties of the time. His next task was his edition of Shakespeare (1725), a work for which he was not well qualified, though the preface is a fine piece of prose. The *Miscellanies*, the joint work of Pope and Swift, were published in 1727 and 1728, and drew a storm of angry comment, which in turn led to the production of *The Dunciad*, first published in 1728. It was published again with new matter in 1729, an additional book – the fourth – being added in 1742. In *The Dunciad* Pope satirised with a wit, always keen and biting, often savage and unfair, the small wits and poetasters, and others of higher quality, who had dealt him real or supposed injuries. Between 1731 and 1735 he produced his *Epistles*, the last of which, addressed to Arbuthnot, is also known as the *Prologue to the Satires*, and contains his ungrateful character of Addison under the name of Atticus; and, in 1733, the *Essay on Man*, written under the influence of Bolingbroke. His last works were his *Imitations of Horace*, published between 1733 and 1739, and the four books of *The Dunciad*.

Pope's position as a poet has been the subject of much contention among critics. There was a reaction against the neo-classicism of his poetry as Romantic tastes began to prevail later in the 18th century, and in the 19th century Pope was often inaccurately dismissed as bitter, malicious, and 'unpoetic' (though Byron, significantly, challenged this view). More recently the quality of his verse has again been recognised. He was the master of the heroic couplet, and in its polish and perfection he aimed to reflect the qualities of the true poet, a seer, a man of taste and dedication, committed to the preservation of human and social standards. These positive qualities lie behind the spleen and bitterness particularly of *The Dunciad* and *The Epistle to Arbuthnot* and they combine to give the mock-heroic vision a genuine touch of elegiac splendour and of tragedy. It is this sense of the poet's committed rôle which gives *The Rape of the Lock*, for all its surface delicacy and apparent triviality, a deep sense of human understanding and sympathy; it also prevents the *Essay on Man*, which is largely a reworking of received wisdom, from falling into complacency or conventionality. His couplets have an epigrammatic quality; 'True wit is nature to advantage dressed/What oft was thought, but ne'er so well expressed', and many of his observations ('A little learning is a dangerous thing') have passed into the language as proverbial.